João Borges da Cunha was born in 1973, in Lisbon, Portugal, where he has been based ever since. He has written fiction, poetry and drama, for which he was awarded a literary prize by the Calouste Gulbenkian Foundation. He holds a degree in architecture, which he also teaches at the university level. He's a scholar of culture. This is his first original, entirely written in English. He is a 'Mary-Jane-Kellyist'. Not a 'Ripperologist'.

For my sister, Sofia
For my son, Romão

João Borges da Cunha

M.J.K's One Hundred Talks on Mary Jane Kelly

AUSTIN MACAULEY PUBLISHERS™

LONDON • CAMBRIDGE • NEW YORK • SHARJAH

A CIP catalogue record for this title is available from the British Library.

ISBN 9781398421615 (Paperback)
ISBN 9781398421622 (Hardback)
ISBN 9781398421639 (ePub e-book)

www.austinmacauley.com

First Published 2022
Austin Macauley Publishers Ltd®
1 Canada Square
Canary Wharf
London
E14 5AA

My familiarity with Mary Jane Kelly's murder and the 'Ripper' case is the result of many readings. I choose to mention only one: Paul Begg's *Jack the Ripper: The Facts*.

This book was also written under the mood of Joseph Conrad's *The Secret Agent*.

The following claim should be put into context. Otherwise, it might gain the cruellest resonance. If it weren't the changing of the normal life brought in by the recent world events, I couldn't have taken the time, as well as, reached the state of mind to pass into written form all the talks, poems and verses that are a part of this book. So, thank you, "new-normal".

Author's Note

Mary Jane Kelly was the last victim of the so-called canonical Whitechapel murders, which were, all the records agree upon, perpetrated by the same individual, supposedly of the male sex, during the second half of 1888. This man was given a sobriquet of such a broad resonance that it became a commonplace in popular culture, and even in the literary milieu as well as in the entertainment industry. It even gave way to a pseudo-discipline, nurtured by curious experts, dogged specialists, detective novel readers, the one was coined after the nickname he became known for: *Ripperology*. Nonetheless, this figure gained the interest of historians, urban sociologists, human geographers, criminologists and psychology profilers, in an extensive production of serious material that helps to understand the epoch, the place, the people and the way they lived. Notwithstanding, the actual facts of the killings were never completely explained, despite the deep commitment of several politicians, police agents, detectives, investigators and doctors at the time. The man was never discovered, found, nor brought to trial. In this way, the historical and popular consensus is that the crimes will remain forever unsolved, what inscribed them in the list of the most puzzling mysteries of modern times. It fell into a myth. The only sure thing about it is that the killer took to the fore a kind of criminals that only almost a century later would get their jargon designation as *serial-killers*.

The murder of Mary Jane Kelly was such a barbaric and extreme deed that it turned the victim, and the circumstances, into a morbid cult event. However, there are other elements in her life and herself that lend particular motives for a literary achievement.

This book is a collection of poems, the fictional author of which, bearing the same initials of the real Mary Jane Kelly, offers the name of "talks". In fact, there isn't any surviving documental subject that could relate directly to Mary Jane Kelly, a piece of garment, a piece of paper, a line of a written note. There's only mediated material, either by the testimonies of people close to her, or by means of police records and newspaper readings. Therefore, in order not to fall in the fetishistic literary device of spectrality and dream imagery about a ghostly person, the only way, so it seems to be by some MJK, is to put Mary Jane Kelly to talk and speak out her mind, so we can listen to her judgements, appreciations, thoughts and even singings. All but fictionally, so to speak. That's why the tone of this book stretches from orally tales to verbal stereotypes, from self-fiction narrative to under-lyrical visions, from drama plots to dialogical lines. Sometimes in a low style, others in a high-spirited mood.

Because it is all about listening to Mary Jane Kelly, her murderer is never heard, and the name which made him a celebrity is never mentioned alike.

The way Mary Jane Kelly was given to death endures such an unhuman and devilish reputation that it isn't a jest to recover the daring Theodor Adorno's dictum which tells that after Auschwitz, no more poetry could be written. Under the same strain, we can tell that after Mary Jane Kelly's murder, no more romantic like lyrical poetry can be achieved. Let's try it otherwise.

JBC João Borges da Cunha 2022

1

Call me Emma Belle,
take me into my yearly ride
from Thrawl Street where I fell
into Miller's Court where I hide.
This is the current year
not the one before.
Could have spent my arrears
on pints, or on some soul of yore.
The fact is that I've chosen thee
just because you have agreed
on a good night sleep, like no whore.
But what a fuss, what a charivari
the morning after you have made free
all the demons, dreams and days.
Either whatever fails off me.

2

Give me an uncle,
my jolly fellow, it can be roughly you, Master,
as long as you scratch my ankle,
as soon as you do it faster and faster,
and bring to a loose my slave bangle.
Juggle out those starry holly daggers
which you bring in your bag-bunker.
Do settle the bungle
of my ever-rolling existence on a caster.
Don't forget the handle,
Bloody master, press it softly either nastier.
Draw me, my good pencil,
Outline me, sculpt me, rip me, conquer a castle
just for me and my angels, moaners outside, crying: we want
Mary Jane Lee.

3

A terrace
it is not.
An embrace
tide of thoughts
made of lace

and shiny pots
painted in aces,
hearts and dots.
It is not.
Hearts of grace
there's a lot,
but out of the race
towards the spot
where my winning pace
will be bitten hot.
Here's the place:
Miller's Court.

4

Never tell much about your story,
Mrs Buki kept repeating, just out north
of the London Docks North Quay.
I wonder, Lady Buki, if there's any glory
in not having high words to pay.
And how to come out forth under no guise of a Penelope
waiting for her master, Mrs Buki.
A mythomaniac, that's my sort.
Incapable of showing a chamber key
as if it would not cast onto a noble door
of some castle by an ancient sea,
despite its actual use in a lousy rookery.
What a telling, Mr Cullen. Thanks thee.
Back to my embroidered lies and Merry Christmas, Mrs Buki.

5. The Virus Inquest – Part I

Have you got a cough,
devilishly devastating
deep in you, Master Builder?
Give me no gob, just stating
facts, like, are you tough
enough to pick me for a guilder,
or is it your voice on grating,
or is that you're just a laugh
quite rough, as that of a sailor
after seven years of standing
out of ladies, girls, no tailor?
Is that what have brought
you back in town on a landing
labelled a zed and two noughts?
Forget the facts, the quarantine, be my suitor.

6

Let us see if you accomplish
the conditions to escort
a pretty buxom girl [Dew *dixit*]
into her table and her dish.
Some say you're the sort of stout, short on words, derelict.
I envision hearsay about it
for years to come, just to finish
on your blow, your notch, your fort.
Come along, Master Builder, do it
as you know how, like a silver fish.
Carry the girl in your loins into her port,
swim slowishly so no alarm gets to it;
swing your fins like knives in the flesh.
It is you who will end up eaten, old sport.

7

Be my most honourable guest.
But I ask you please, shut up
the spell on me. I do dare use
to cover the lanes, uncover my breast,
discover my pal, and no charming up.
I see, you know, I mean, can you excuse,
despite my *considerable personal best*,
the fact that the one worthy fact is a cup
on spirits, for me and me only. No abuse,
I know, you see. They shout, get to rest,
Otherwise, you'll end up being cheered up
by a mischievous fellow, one on disabuse
of me, who on his part will shut his chest
with all of his forgery. You're not that kind of chap.
Are you? Am I? Pay it right now my fuse. Will you?

8

A delivery:
what had
the streets
made of me?
I am glad
I do agree
I pay a fee
to all the sad
but noisy fleet
of needy
folks, bad
on sore feet,
on greedy
shores, no bed
just me, Black Maree.

9

Ought to speak my perspicuous mind.
Haven't really run the streets till I met
my dear Master Builder, a clever man.
Words in mouth of the feverous kind
he had not, just the promise of a bet:
He would offer me one shiny gold can
if I'd prove to him my obnoxious find,
that he's done Annie, and Elizabeth,
Cathy and Mary Ann. But what a man.
No proof. Just the terrible, vicious bind
to a suspicion of mine, fancy Jeanette,
whose further thoughts, abashed by a fan
of jeepers creepers, drew shut the blinds.
I no longer see who you are, my cat.
Now, ever in the dark, I'll give you the ban.

10

I shall explain
this again.
Fair Emma
for female
subpoena.
Mary Jeanette
for the ones
in regret.
Ginger Kelly,
Black Mary.
Behold what
the streets
have made of me,
a school of characters
forlorn in the sea.

11

Looking through the looking glass
I see a bunch of seers seeing through
a crystal ball, no less than a glass of beer
no other than Olympia, the bar, where
a glass of this worths as much as glass
of that, right there where the looking glass
has turned somehow into a mirror of you.
Suddenly the future was coming through
the looking glass, right before me, however
beyond it. Pecking gently on my heels
there you were, sure were, but where, but how?
I turned my back to the looking glass
and faced the deserted Fashion Street
opposite Olympia – there again your sorcery
which you exert between the two, vanishing whatever
through.

12

When in here
I was only one.
That was London
nothing close
nothing near.
Rambling
Mary Jane
heading
Brick Lane
for some shoes.
Best of luck, Miss Jeanette,
I can see you have surely been
to France and no doubt to Italy too.
Since then and for times unforeseen
I were to be masterly two.

13

Men were gaming the workers' game
which consists in keeping a hand on the wheel
and the blink of one eye on a passer-by's high heel.
Yet it used leading to the fate of a lame.
A gammy hand smashed on some speed gear,
The eye crooked by the look of the dame
who in the end was a vulgar witch to blame
for selling nothing but rotten fruit and some fear.
These are the Whitechapel days. As for the nights,
let me put the plot all the way around the sights.
Women were playing the hooker's play
which consists in parading along a stretch
of Dean Street, seeking for customers to fetch.
Then a rusty voice entertains, "Will you?" What a say.

14

When you pick up a lover named Joe
it's better if he turns out to be a Yankee,
and even better if he turns to be a foe
of all the old school porters with a key
to the Spitalfields Market and the Kews.
My Joe didn't like me to have a Julia
in my room. But I loved Julia as I was
fond of Joe, not the Yankee, but the Joe
of Irish Christian breeding, Hallelujah.
If my Joe were from American brow,
It would be splendid to him that two
happy girls like Jane and Julia slept tight
together up to one, only one misty night.
And a morning, and a day. And when the sun
would rise in America, my Joe there, would wave high:
I adore you Julia-Jane.

15

Letter from Mary Kelly:
Man Joe, whatever you still do,
don't you do wrong and turn out
as you've told I did, leaving you
behind, out of our number thirteen.
Children to be, straight from your semen
and me, out of my womb down to you,
are waiting for a delivery, and shouting
on the streets to what they'll hunger.
A house, a room, a bed, one chamber.
As soon as we expand to number
twenty-six Dorset Street, and raze
the partition to the shed, what a mansion.
Note from Joe Barnett's (*Answer*):
Have you talked to the Master Builder?

16

Went to Mrs Phoenix's, Bow Common Lane.
Just to talk it over and tell her that the portion
Barnett was no longer my close companion.
Why is that, Miss Kelly? Loose the Mary Jane
in you, and back to Emma, Ginger, Jeanette,
and all other characters knitted in your net.
The streets do want them, moreover the Dorset,
that pitfall of poor devils, where he'll be again,
pauper Joe. Making use of his porter's cane
to drive the cattle into the Christ Church jest.
Then you'll say, what a customer, what a talent
so well-built, then you'll overlook he's Barnett.
A priest into your life, wouldn't you vent?
Wouldn't you breathe deeper, stripping your vest?
I guess not, Mrs Phoenix, Joe's in Advent.

17

I lingered on looking around to Tower Hamlets
while my former landlord's sister-in-law kept
ironing, kept dusting, kept saying her prayers.
She'd listen to me for hours of grey and greyer
light of the day, with an eager hear to doom.
I've told you already, Marie Jeanette, loom
your considerable personal attractions which
are yours, only yours, and forget about a groom.
Roam the streets. Try a Lodging House, some rich
and tidy one up Brick Lane or Mile End Road.
By all means, dear sister-in-law, I do own a room,
Thirteenth, Miller's Court. No less, Mrs Phoenix.
Just need an old chap to move in with me to twenty-six.
Take care, Marie, some boomer is helping others
with their inner walls. No fear, sister dear, on the Master
Builder.

18

The highest thing about having a Mrs Phoenix
around is not what they all tell, the girls,
tell and desire, the wish of an esquire. Nix! Nix!
Lady Phoenix is no protector, no brothels
manager, no bedding house tough Circe.
Nor a confessor by the burden of your sins.
She's a Matrix Builder, like the Master one.
What is it worth for, my friends, keeping
secrets, taking whispers, fleeing the battle,
just to live a few more hours as the saddle
of a bully, that of a lord, our kingdom's eave?
I myself have put the pudenda on a leave,
and do simply employ the pituitary. I snore
in a daydream about cushions. Want to cheat
on life. Once. Mrs Phoenix says either more.

19

There's little in a life composed so much,
so clocked, as the one under the horns
coming from the Thames. There's no such
sound of choke to offer a day of corns
to the peacocks corded in Aldgate stores.
They'll remain there plucked by the touch
of a seagull's love, of a seagull's gush.
And the seagull chants a chant of river shores;
it sounds a little like someone on a slush,
where peacock and seagull are ever whores.
Forever. One on a master's leash, no lore.
The other fleeing the river to shit on a bush
by Rope Walk Gardens. Deep there, mud's
no inconvenient; peacock tastes its odour,
seagull's fond to deliver. A still life to adore.
Master composes the better, comes and cuts
the throat of the two.

20

When I was your age, Jeanette, times weren't mine.
I did search for them, Marie, but ended losing my age.
Don't be my age ever again, Mary Jane, your spine
will try to look timeless, Kelly girl, but time's no sage
bringer, it only pretends to be so, Ginger; I did engage
with so many fellows, Fair Emma, and time was a supine
engine to rollover; just the scant of days on a burnt pine.
My suitors were all gentlemen, wanton of the page
written in Trafalgar Square, on such a Sunday red line.
Lost my age, never found the times, see the disgrace.
I envisage the times, Mrs Phoenix, like age eaters.
that's a rush thing to think, Mrs Phoenix, an outlet
saying to say, Mrs Phoenix, but the constable beaters
are not into philosophy, Mrs Phoenix, I have no seaters
to rest, that's the meaning of time; do bury me in Tower
Hamlets.

21

This much possessed by thoughts so many
that Commercial Street became my shadow
screen, our river of shades, where a swallow
is taken for a seagull, where girls so steady
quickly dissolve into expired meat so foul,
that a brain is no longer the mind's bowl.
Let me tell you about these thoughts' heady
visions. Mrs Phoenix discards their verity.
And I say to her, they are not about ages,
They're only the truth of Mary Jane Kelly's
pleasant notions on gowns and nighties.
Never wear shawls other colour than blackies
As you run the Strand after eight, Mr Phoenix
rebukes. I never go that far, sister, my fancies
are all about how to fix Master's look on trendies.

22

See that building, it looks like my mother. Or other.
Let me confess, it is not the cladding *finishments*,
She was exquisite all the way through garments
no one could detach from straw, which was loather
and drier each child delivered, every payment
expired. The building, as you see, is being devoured
by mouldy creepers, put down into a green flavoured
wreckage that doesn't even save the basements.
But it makes an enchanting ensemble with the garden,
and a combination even happier to skirts coloured
many, from the bunch of women entering their burden.
Some of them in blue, thinking of Venus and Saturn,
some of them in red, with their minds on pennies, no bother;
Some of them in yellow, fixed in being on good terms
with the landlord or lady. They're the building germs.
Those were what dwelled within her, just colours.
My mother, no other.

23

Taking a ride into the district, just to walk it over,
I passed Flower and Dean Street only for a jest.
Could have gone until fifty-six, that brazen crest
by the name of "White House", but I had no cover.
Things were stumbling in a sinking evening, and don't quite
know, ever, when neighbourhoods become dark
streams full of the most mysterious mysteries of the night,
dreams of the insane and drunken, everyone in a lurk.
They're trying a cheap alchemy of turning black into white
and a house into a hanger of people dying *nightly in their
beds, wringing the hands of ghostly confessors*. All in stitched
clads that no woman would approve and whose alchemical
cleaning taste is bound to Sulphur. That's when the streams
come deep clear
One glimpses their bottom, from where emerges the Master's
gleam, a Neptune's tail. I claim, kill! States he: *There will be
time to murder and create.*

24

Have to run, the lizard is dead.
Mrs Cox's news.
Elizabeth Prater's kitten went ahead
and took no few
blows on poor lizard's neck.
I had him so newly
accommodated in his glass vivarium
with stones he tuned
like a god moving the mountains,
a centaur in a crewed
Crystal Palace, which I fostered
for the sake of whim.
I mean, for the sake of a hope
to offer the Master Builder
an atmosphere of quaint and dope.

25

I went down through Hanbury
and found it this upturned and swivelled.
How can you figure up a murky
assassination in a place so dishevelled
by moves of machines on curdy
sewers, that my pacing became unlevelled?
Thus my feet were thinking, cruelly,
Could damned Chapman have lightheaded
chosen such a spot, this silly,
that cruising down there should be just tightened?
She chose progress and billy
beats, she chose where the city wasn't fastened.
No detectives had it goodly,
now that the city has lost itself into scrambled
eggs. From start to end I'd been shuffled.

26

It was Whitechapel High, can't quite remember.
Some sort of claret had been mellowing my veins,
and each separate dying ember was in drains
upon a stream of vinegary water, which, I temper,
was a trace of the watery part of the world.
In the middle of the dry cobblestones ground
I did march like a soldier obeying harsh words
to move on, to go up, to never look backwards.
Sure did I. But suddenly I trampled some pound
parcelled in a piece of rag, so tender that a found
like that couldn't remain an unadmired award,
simply thrown upon the floor. Picked it up to my ward.
The result: as it opened, a dirty napkin was wrapping up a pair
of lively eyes, ripped out from face sockets, both looking
upward at me. I paid back the look. Certainly not *the end of*
the affair.

27

At Commercial and Leman crossing, a school of fellows
made a battalion ring entirely about my figure;
the circle wasn't much of a great wall. More of a lure
drawn by spotted panthers; gobblers; in their mellow
and throaty voices they claimed for a protector,
not a prey. I say. They wanted a temple, a stage,
and in its core the central eyes of a Marie Lloyd
singing afore anthems of the revolution and rage.
I did the folklore instead; sang the fields, the void
and silent Limerick hills, and the Shannon's gurgle,
where I come from. My eyes were in the parcel,
inside my pocket. And I tightened them so sensible,
that I felt they danced between hand and fingers,
like two gruesome pets, eager to see the limelight singers.

28

The amphitheatre of men offered such an attuned applause,
That the singing lesson seemed to had risen up their hope
of reaching a joyous living, that of an easier savour to cope
with; seed, heed, feed, all much chanting indeed. Don't pause,
he said, Marie, Marie, hold on tight, on your voice, your eyes.
My pocketed globes, two nervous gems no easy to dispose?
Thus shouted a beautiful brute that had come forth: give us a
bow,
Marie of the prairies, our Holy Marie from Paris and White's
Row.
Piece by piece, the street show had been on the move to
Wentworth.
So thoroughly arranged as if a procession on a worship of a
figure: I.
In the meantime, the mob started crying for a stall, it would
be worth it, if we all could try your lap. Sell us a stall, Marie,
the one on your lap.
As one of the eyes in my pocket bit my leg, the poor brute had
kissed me by the eye; this daring put the men to knock one
another as if a rap
had been robbed from *the Temple of Broken Stones*. Class
dismissed.

29

Had to run from that school.
The singing was majestic,
but my ears were frying fool;
my four eyes under frenetic
spinning, the ones in their socket
and the odd ones in my pocket.
The latter looked like beaming
a laugh much bizarre, a yowling
so ghastly that I longed for a doctor.
Those jewelleries, a *theft by finding,*
which I'd much shielded, were they mocking?
Right behind, a man of the mob came
after me; was that it? I took the lived eyes
out of the cloth, and once in the flesh of my hand
they turned into two crippled stones. Dead.
Then in grand style I threw them backwards.
Hey, Miss, you've almost killed me with those eyes.

30

It would be the most dramatic gesture
that I were to be submitted to, and should stay put,
Mrs Phoenix said; and she was as sure
as a column raised upon the Strand, it's absolute.
What is that Mrs Phoenix, now turned
into Mrs Column, if you will? I got undermined;
not by the suggestion, or else by the future
deed, but by the secret, she stated, that must be assigned
to what my past days would certainly ensure: something dirty.
It was more of a hiding, truly, than some grotesque secrecy,
she reaffirmed. What is that painstaking thing all about
Doctor Phoenix?
Clean colours. Let's wash that topsy-turvy hair of yours Mary
Jane, and give back
to the world what earth can´t offer, what fire can't either fix,
what air can simply mess, what only boiled water can touch.
What images return, O my daughter.
Then the opaline blond ginger
Chastain glow of each thread on
your head will guide you under
ether along the Strand line.

31

Once again, a building is staring at me as if exhibiting its genitalia,

in such a manner that it looked like I should be that responsible

for not having given back its colours to the streets, the city & *alia;*

either to cleaners which could render its iridescent grey visible;

for good. Everybody inside was in an uproar about barbarisms committed under the buildings' eyes. It couldn't testify to nothing.

This, sure, made it an enraged piece to talk to, with its monism of smoke, ashes, cement and whatever is paler among pale things.

I was transforming myself into a "flâneuse", was that it? An illness

worse than the pox, which makes you talk to your own talks and wait

for questions and answers, even from the building's cinder madness.

It asked, "Will I see you no more before eternity?"; you with your bait, did retaliate, *O you whom I would have loved, O you who knew it!*

I've given a look back to that schizoid monument and what a bore,

the only colour that I glimpsed was the ginger shade of hair there before.

32

It stands on one side, Christian Street, of that I can be certain.
I do recognize my folly in going back to look the grizzly house
in the face. Perhaps to tell it, we were of the very same rouse
of moods, and that between us there was only a misty curtain
of messy hair, a little atmosphere of keeping our distances;
a snobbish way of hiding our ill state. As for it, its fishy estate
condition. As for me, my liver disease, giving me the trances.
I finally found it, now much less burdened on its façade of
taste a bit Teutonic, highly Plutonic; with no filthy articles to
display, just a sallow gable and an eave helmet trying to be of
the radiant kind, up the middle of such a bleak ensemble of
people in rampant cry for another sacrificed girl. There it was,
a Cretan temple clay to the brim of becoming mired under a
pool of much poured out tears.
The house, no move. And I sort of felt invited to the exequies
in the rears.
I peered back there, and saw the Master Builder. Let's get into
this play.

33

It turned all to be the other way round.
As I envisaged the house helmet,
a twinkle of the most thrilling set
hit my eyesight; therefore, I found
that the building had a foppish eye,
so provoking that it might be worth
an excision. Stealing that gem cried
for braveness or for this boldly forth
a way of cunny hands or a sly brain.
Was it Murano, or an *oculus* window?
Colours of such a hypnotic strain,
that the sanguine mixed with yellow.
Come along here and help me out,
I did call upon the Master Builder
in the rear. Shall we rip that stone down?

34

I shall restate. It was a sombre building
of an imposing countenance, but a declining
allure. I was quite sure it was a mortuary
in Christian domain, full of moans, dreary
clamours, and funereal exhibition of limbs,
lips in *rigor mortis* and rotten cheekbone.
It insisted in showing the sexual organs
down from the basements up to the nimbus.
However, in its highest spot there was this stone
so rare, that I would kill one of its dead ladies
to take it into my possessing. Climbing up, crazies
and deviant ones, I did balance on Master's
shoulders, he on his heels, to straightly reach the treasure,
a bloody eye worth taking onto to bed just for pleasure.
A Caryatid upon an Atlas. How funny was that? As I touched
the eye, it all fell to pieces, broken cobblestones on the street
ground.

35

We've arranged to meet
the four of us at the corner
between East Commercial Road
and low Jubilee Street.
The deed would be to avenge
those poor four and make a toad
of that killer prince whose tinge
of a kiss tastes like a lethal load
of bloody spit and knives on a hinge.
Marie Jeanette came from the west.
Fair Emma arrived from the east.
Ginger Marie walked from Musbury.
Black Maria climbed the Sutton.
We've made a *Parcae* chorus to button
back to life Mary Ann, Annie, Liz and Cathy. Mary Jane Kelly
went missing.

36

Neatly, nicely, by disbelief or bridges
unsafe on the crossing, a revenge,
beautiful in the designing of ridges
and grooves, goes beyond a bondage;
it is to be an undertaking of hooves
that will smash the cursed toad's
mouth. This a note sent by wolves
biting Kelly's mind, barking roads,
eyeless houses and lockdown
hearts. What do you mean by ridges,
crafty Jane? She sent in the doves,
flying up in the shape of a crown;
they all yelled a froggy libel about
dead hands, dead stringencies.
Only birds can fetch the beasties.

37

The Kelly's four of hers
 walked towards Queen's Head
public house. Sorcerers
heading north, not to their beds,
but to their claim to lynch
the amphibious vagabond
and bring him under a *pendulum*.
The doves cut off the binge
as they entered the royal Head;
Emma, Marie, Maria and Mary
made such a havoc that led
all men to step back to the terry
walls as if in a line of fire.
The witches shouted, Hang
the froggeries in a wire.

38

Kelly's infuriated gang
did they declare in a pang,
No rest, grin out your fangs
arrest, scarf, kill, they sang.
Did they keep over. Feet
on the bar between dishes
forks and knives, kinky kicks
upon spoons and benches;
they were standing on the marble lid
in a fiend parade, sure they did.
The doves' beating wings to infinity
initiated a draught tuned to their queer
psalm, Recover MALC's dignity, it just is.
One sirrah, held to the wall, exuding fear,
didn't he hardly ask, "Which political party is this?"

39 Day [-] 7

Sorry Miss,
a shy laddie
approached.
Are you Marie
Jeanette, from
Dorset Street?
A smart youth
with a fleet
voice to the
matter, just
a petty pinch
on his lows,
pretending
the raw adult
he still wasn't. Sure, I am, warrior dear.

40 Day [-] 6

Sorry Miss,
a lad, boldly
though moody,
did come near.
Are you Marie
Jeanette, from
Dorset Street?
He besieged
me like a stone
pillar buried
in a plastered
hole, down
the pavement.
Around I went
and kept my
passing by. Voice of joy, sad pinch, Are you?

41 Day [-] 5

Dear Miss,
a lad came by.
I looked at him,
right from the high
of my highest self.
Did he seriously
make the question?
Are you Marie
Jeanette, from
Dorset Street?
A tenor colour
to his talk with a gust.
I kept walking by
though I sensed
he had stopped. Gained my trust, Just from March to August.
Thank you.

42 Day [-] 4

My respectable Dame;
 much more a lad than
the ones before him,
or was he the same rogue,
now three pages older?
This time I knew better.
I stretched out my hand
and gave it to him for
a greeting gesture.
He took it in his own
and kissed it in a bone
so chastely, that he made
no sound. What a silence.
I didn't let him into further questions.
To no avail. In a crystal tone, Are you, milady, Miss Marie
Jeanette from Dorset Street?

43 Day [-] 3

The crystal lad and I,
we walked down
Goulston and then
back up Middlesex,
shoulder to shoulder.
From the onset, I
did offer him a serious
response,
Mary Jane Kelly
From Miller's Court,
How do you do?
The crystal-made boy
did not quiver, nor did he
even reveal a vibration.
Greetings replied, he just poignantly twinkled, Are you a
prostitute?

44 Day [-] 2

The Crystal and the Ginger,
they weren't just on a promenade,
were they? A swollen finger
hurt in between, like pomegranate
grains stuck within roughly peel.
People lose their chances
looking not in the eye; to the heel;
pour of tor and distances.
The Crystal did blink in a bashful
line, Do not have the prick
for you, Miss. Ginger gulped a full
hand of guffaws, one brick,
two teeth, three bones, four Maries. Retorts, no lack,
I'm more into diamonds, clubs, spades and hearts.
Crystal tried his luck, And what is your trump jack?

45 Day [-] 1

Do you think, Miss Ginger, a tree
does prostitute itself?
Crystal was a defiant lad to feed
on tricks, a gauzy elf.
Ginger did. Do you figure
what is beyond the canopy of leaves,
under the tree trunk, among the eaves
of branches? Roots, a deep lure.
Roots that exchange, for a small change,
the sap and the nectar within the grange.
Yes, they sell themselves, no cure.
Do you think, Miss Ginger, buildings do also prostitute
themselves?
The glass manikin didn't quit the query.
Goodbye, Crystal. Farewell, Mary Kelly.

46

People, they say, *know a little of Mary Kelly's*
movements during the week I've been driven into the red eye,
couched in my *cauldron of morning*.
I'm not supposed to talk of it. am I? – It was given
me the privilege to walk along in a ghostly laddie's
company. Perhaps it was not only that, an evening
event of a street woman meeting a street boy, even
more prodigal than the eldest brother of all gods.
Let me tell you what it was, for the sake of memory,
of him, trees, buildings and me; the sake of testimony
of sold nectar in every dead root's inquest; of nods
paltry offered to both of us by passers-by in agony.
I was Ginger Girl he was Crystal Laddie. How could
I foster such a vitreous boy within me, where crowds
of Joes and Julias are having a fight? Ginger and Crystal,
Broken glasses.
The Master Builder has promised to glue the boy together
for the future's sake; just some rays of death.
He would become a hyacinth in Master's head.
Sorry, Miss, did you say Crystal Lady?

47

Today it was lizard's burial day.

I wanted it done in Tower Hamlets.

Could have not left Elizabeth's kitten, lizard's killer to linger at bay.

Come on, you murderer, bring your holder. Assassin cat and its owner to the grave.

Joe Barnett came along, acting the brave,

What for did you put a lizard by the shoulder,

didn't it cause you any fright, any distress?

Demented Barnett caught my stern temper,

It wasn't an it, it was a he, and all tenderness.

…ness, Mary Jane? A reptileness member.

Listen insensate man, He was in my utmost adore.

…dore, Marie? Have you turned into a snake charmer?

Barnett's echolalia, got to my nerves. All out – my roar.

…oar.

48

The lizard's funeral hour.
Mary Jane Kelly, embittered
carer of the deceased pet,
paced the contrite train
of mourners. Elizabeth's
kitten carried, on its back,
the lizard's shroud, all made
of orange skin bandages.
Barnett, an oar on his back
to dig the grave. No shovel.
…ovel? Didn't he just forget?
At Tower Hamlets there were
guards and gardeners on every square
feet. A hole in the lawn? Barely ever.
The lizard's corpse ended up thrown down
the water of the Regent's Canal, much to
Miss Kelly's dismay, Go my lizard, go conquer the Thames.
…ames. Amen.

49

I came across Morganstern, an old companion,
How long has it been? For watershed floods,
too much of that since the rainfall canyon
has been drained into thirsty streets of blood.
Have you finally completed your education,
Dear M. Jane? – With Morganstern I've attended
all the courses on dark scarves, incantation
and black semi opaque skirts, right to those ended saints'
days, when the seagulls fought the pheasants,
the turkeys strangled the peacocks; and the doves
shited the whole festival. There was no sky, just ants,
bugs and worms which have learnt how to fly above
the two. We've lived a delusional faith upon the whole.
As if the East End were in a beginning and not on a blatantly
fireworks ending. Spell *cockroach*, spell it just for me Janelly.

50

I was trying to guess
which one of them
I did know the best.
Or had an interest
on offer her a gem.
Wasn't particularly
 fond of this donnish
 Countess Godiva,
due to her party
on being a diver
in cold Coventry,
one horse driver,
a bad taste for white,
one worse for nudity.
I do miss the Stride.

51

La Stride, *aka* Long Liz,
can't avoid it, did always
cause me the bad envies.
Chic, she gave the sways
that even a deserted street
is much bound to observe.
Didn't know her that good,
quite a gazelle out of retreat.
A cherry, sure she deserves.
Saw her these days, a *rood*
sticked down her veiling hood.
La Eddowes gives me the hell.
She was blatant, she was brave,
adored. From me, an asphodel.
Saw her today getting in a cave.

52

La Chapman, *aka* Dark Annie
had no scent for dark danger.
Met her like a mother, the Baroness
of the "Ringers"; came to me, no feigner,
Do always bring a shawl, you fairness.
Now, just can't see her anymore out
of the yard in Chapmanbury for Hanbury.
From the Wilkes Street corner, I sort
of figured some figure coming from
twenty-nine, but in such a spectrally made
shape, and so many times in a row, that
I've just perceived how many Chapmans
did live there, within her, inside her body,
and who were now deserting the most
tearful corpse I have ever seen. A ring.

53

I longed for Crystal to come along.
The Crystal Lad of my last week.
My Crystal boy and me, a caprice.
I've even intoned one baiting song,
but the streets, in their November
noise, have made of my voice a puff
and have shattered every member
of the Crystal Chap. Got a muff
and went alone crystaless to see
Buck's Row. Didn't ever heard
of her, La Nichols, but I had a bee
telling me that she was a bird
for the ignored. The Buck's spot cried
the truth. She just needed a door.
I bid her a platinum gate. Crystal died.

54

I do not doubt
that I must be
some gouge,
lifting memory
after mystery
for the sake
of a mission
to undertake.
Just a scission
it is, scuffing
at Mary Jane's
oneness, suffering
the possession
of my cruellest
sixth version.

55

Rambling from the "Ten Bells"
straight to the "Blue Coat Boy",
into the "Horn of Plenty", coy
harbour of the ones who sell,
What do they sell? Back
to "Britannia" where a stall
is ever there, an empty sack
waiting for my soring gall.
Have you got the coins,
girl? What for? I wondered.
This lad led me to my ruins.
Have you got the sour liver,
Miss girly? I'm just this *noisy
in liquor*, otherwise, a very
quiet woman to take to deliver.

56

Up to the core of the centre of evil,
some crossing between Dorset
and Commercial Street, an inset
of all the greatest insensible ones.
Nonetheless, it was, in short, my play,
going back to the "Britannia", where
I do belong, don't I? Try not to dismay,
though full of ghosts within me, Fair
whatever I used to be named for.
Have you got the coins, girl? Had I
not heard of this request right before?
Are you, Miss, the sad kind of a bore?
I'm into jokes; I can ease you, can't I?
Please don't. I'm only into myths and ghosts.
I can do that, Miss, wait for the next talk. I'll host.

57

What are you made of,
what are you made for?
Mostly just to jerk off,
Miss, but I'm also ashore
for the sake of nasty jokes,
right to cheer up some gore
of a lady whose hair chokes
the plenty of other carnivals
in her. Most touched, Sailor,
Will you leap up some intervals
in between? Seats or pallors,
Miss? – let me get into it, anyhow,
Why was it a black horse that Lady Godiva
fetched for her ride? Because God had hived
all the white whores. Have you still got the black saliva?

58

A white ceremonial, which I use to call
the Whitechapel's *solemnis mass,*
consists of bringing out a stool for a stall
in the crossing of Sutton and Martha's,
and seat to see the throng lost in the all.
By my side a bundle of peeled glass.
Then as I start the quaint liturgical ball
in a silence smile, an odour of carcass;
some bow at me, as if to an ancestral
Caryatid fallen from a building's ass.
Others sense that I'm a priestess girl
to despise. Thereby, the blessed lass
doesn't spare anyone and gives a fall
of putrid fruits, bitten lumps, a high pass
out of the sack, thrown at hand to each pal.

59

I've been tartly running out of dreams.
The mental and the other lively ones,
those which lead a girl to her screams
for gravellier days, even more in tone
with the Whitechapel bleakest hours.
Had thrown rotten onions to the smokers,
the men in the "Cradle of Liberty", pretty
Jews; two weeks long pears in the greedy
face of Clay Pipe Alice, the one protector
to the district; even my adored Master Builder
had I hit with a foul banana's smelly peel,
poor goon, has he done anything amiss to iller
people than myself, whose dreams offer a feel
of rooms too littered, of flames too close to a killer?
In a nutshell, my deserted dreams are simply that of an eel.

60

Why do you throw fruit on people,
is that any good to recover from a life
the fancies of which are just feeble
strings of kinship with ales, a knife,
a shawl, and roamers to the lodgings,
down Flower and Dean Street, a sewer?
I see Bryant up north, there goes a king
Worth of some oranges down his brewer
vest. There I got a *Prince of Orange, bing.*
I watch Levenson, in his pawn shop,
rendering back Isaacs' pearled violin,
and thus it goes one rotten tangerine
for each. There I take a Cupid hop
to see those two old men in cupidity,
temple vendors. They do lend hope
to my reverie.

61

As to each diaphanous
mate who still crosses
my quiet but outrageous
last days, they're in losses
of groceries and rot.
They should all flee.
However, I know not
how to conceal in me
the bullets I've been
saving to exorcise
them and my spleen.
As to Crystal, I'll offer twice
his diamond flesh.
As to Nichols, a ruby Christ.
To the Master Builder, just ice.

62

Paupers with paupers war upon naught.

However, they persist.

I do the sightseeing on them, their fraught mind on vice and mist

made of envied rooms and chestnuts' waste; like last year's snow

they do insist to spare, the poor ones' taste to a phantasy grown

upon the eighty years' war, when each William had a domain to shut.

Surely a Whitechapel like district, the East Ham Advertiser, or the cut

made by Regent's Canal onto the Mile End banks.

Further, the world on cuffs;

The destitutes agree upon these sweetening junk.Coy.Does not joy delights in joy?

63

Entering Dorset Street.
Time and again a ruined return.
I hear within, some friendly nun's
voice, neither chaste nor burnt
by the bloody reputation of a deed
done as a rehearsed role. A blunt
move. Why a nun, why me? A creed.
Is all this a superstition chasing
my short train of thoughts to the brim
of an undreamt-of living? I do listen
to her clinging this flabbergasted
by all the woes on that face of mine.
From which side have you come in
fair maiden, Commercial or Crispin?
Should have answered, but no one's
ever a nun.

64

After all, Dorset Street is no Dorset is no Dorset.

My superstitions are not that superstitious.

Crystal is not that gone as he's been just dead.

Dear lizard has fought Diddles his murderer as he did, he did.

Long Liz has eaten grapes, as grapes have been eaten.

McKenzie was a lady smoker, as she was a lady smoker.

Fruits thrown to passers-by are not thrown fruits, are no fruits.

Barnett's echolalia is not that nonsense, sense, sense, sense.

My education is not an education, not an education.

The chants I don't sing are chants I don't sing, I don't sing.

An evening in "Britannia" is an evening in "Britannia", in "Britannia".

An appalling apron is not that appalling, not that appalling.

Whitechapel usen't to be what Whitechapel was, Whitechapel is.

A murder usually is a try is a try, a try is a try is a try, a tried murder. The Master Builder, he's the man, is the man, is the man, the man he'll be.

65

To the great detachment and bate
of the red eyed bosses, who tremble
for little children's savour, for a mate
in the beddings and *each separate*
 dying ember sparkling in a fire emblem.
To the great damage of their trick's rate,
and their business losses on fake gems;
the scaffolding destined to decapitate
the Boleyn is ghastly being assembled
up Dorset, just where the street ends.
Victoria should have been more considerate
in not allowing such an injurious punishment.
To kill a woman in Whitechapel's core?
I waited for my namesake Seymour
in amusement. Crystal appeared from Kent.

66

The Ghosts' maid
has done this task
beyond compare.
She had been afraid
and didn't want to ask.
In the least, to spare
them to a denial of aid.
Her will: one to bask
each kin ghost in a fair
place for a life laid
down in a hermetic flask.
Known, her Ginger hair.
The thing, her ardour
to accomplish a favour.
Every ghost into a diamond labour,
she said.
Known, her Jane name.
For good, her soubriquet,
Lady Gist.

67

A certain Sir Alfred took all by himself
the relentless endeavour of climbing
Aldgate, Spitalfields and the outskirts,
to reach our court. He was a curious
fellow, full of engines to capture what
he called the motion pictures. In short,
some sort of impostor of which Dorset
is a hived wall. We've known the type,
but didn't understand his language
made of planes, sequences, footage,
frames, some travellings. And settings.
A mesmerizer trying his luck in the real
estate affairs. Unfortunately, he didn't
quite engage into the business. We got
it all, when he insisted in the rear views and the rear windows.
There's nothing like rears in here; we're all in front
of each other, I mocked.
Sir Alfred, welcome to a court, this is not a backyard.
He stared at me and mumbled,
Your hair has the right colour,
however, you are not the perfect Kelly.

68

Spleen again
Ghosts astray
Fruits stain
Crystal ashtray
Talks failed
Nichols ailed
McKenzie sailed
Brick Lane's ale
Lady Godiva freezes
Eddowes seized
Hell's stewed
Murder sewed Mrs Phoenix's sigh
Master Builder's cry.
Let us go I and I.

69

We're on the verge
of some a time passage.
Can you merge
along with me, in a carriage,
black velvet cushions
tumbling up Leman Street?
For the sake of illusions,
let's belittle the fall within it,
that of the light's glaze.
That of a night coming apace
to the event where,
Crystal, I beg you, be my lace.
Since I am unaware
of its repercussions, its embrace,
its broken glass bits down the final face,
the Master Builder is to be
my maze's thread.

70

An Unreal City,
that to which
I do insist to
belong.
Foreigner.
A Coventry
like pool,
too wan
for a girl
and a swan.
Drowned out.
Humans sold
to Equidae;
horses in
butchers' hands
alike.

71

La Prater lets her Diddles,
lizard's killer kitten, and else's,
walk across her naked neck,
just for the tail's sake, I guess.
I'd rather sail to Inverness
In a snake's saddle and peck
the fish in her mouth every sea
mile. Finally, I'd get the scarlet
scot fever and would sail back,
grabbed by a murderer's wrists,
stuck in furred cuffs and hearty
ties. He says, Let's kill that cat,
stop the feline warming, Lady Gist,
and toss the Prater to her priest.
Dear Elizabeth, have another cup,
this is the "Blue Coat".

72

When me and Barnett arranged a room,
some joyful phenomena came to appear.
He just did offer to be my eternal groom,
which has overturned me into Lady Fear.
For long nights, geese stick their beaks
into the shed wall next to the furniture.
They make a drumming like architecture
upon taps of rummy dreams' dead leaks.
By dawn, Mrs Cox takes a coxy tenure,
she runs outside and hunts a Lady Goose.
Caught by the neck, plumes on the loose.
At lunch, we all had some silent nurture.
My bed aspires to be a Londonian bed;
rays much striped light it from the shed
as if it were Miles and Flora's tower of fancy.
I decide to wed the "Horn of Plenty".

73

Going into the shed,
a place I've avoided
to these very days,
the understanding
of Dorset's bays
comes through
this odd a handing
given by a cruel
ground floor.
A marble disgust.
This is not just
about sex and liquor.
But I see now
 beasts with beasts war
for the worst. And before
my bed's wall, I search for the geese.
The partition.
None. No ease. No getting out. Grease
all around, mixed with small much tender
lumps give me the goosebumps; render
the steps hard to resume. I'm in an eon.
Outside there it is: some putrid pigeon
on the skewer of my shoes' high hills.

74

Tell us all about the centre of evil
Marie Jeannette. Let just me clean
my shoes first, I've just arrived
from an enigmatic carnage scene.
And I'd better not squander
 my reputation of a *shabby genteel*
girl *in her attire with considerable*
personal attractions.
But *not a notorious character.*
I've always been fond of inquest
testifying, since nothing is concluded
until they see the diamond stones
within one's kidneys, not in the brains.
Then my beautiful pit, it will be exalted.
There is it: *act so there is no use in a centre.*

75

In between Commercial and Crispin Streets
there's a void to which the well-to-do people
offer a name no other than the *lowest of all*
prostitutes' pit. They do forget that a kernel
it's where the bee queen lives about, almost a nest,
mostly a core. No well, no basin, definitely a crest.
That narrow throne to the drunken is called Dorset.
This tight stone pavement, a costermongers' set
is to be envisage as no hollow; a podium instead.
Every time I do get to Dorset, I can't help suffering
of this megalomania that leads me to see an interior
mahogany staircase, which I climb, rising to the highest
of my fosse, my core, my court. Ginger bee, Kelly Queen.
The shawl, tied up. It gives me the confidence of an insect.
My buzzing begins. I'm sure heaven dwells up here, correct?

76

Does any sunlight get through my window panes?
Spent all day ruminating about the fact.
If I could tell either northward from southward, or grains'
growth from leaves' tinge and tact,
perhaps some illumination would come to my mind.
In that case, no sunlight I should need.
Sunny hours would glow from within to divinely blind my
eyes of a moth on circles of greed.
I went out by eleven in the morning after awaken at ten.
If I could tell either it was me from someone else,
 or elsewhere from the street where you live, in self-pity then
I would have not lingered, measuring my hasty pulse
each time I crossed from pavement to pavement.
The day is already at an end Miss Kelly, can I make any
arrangement? It was closing time in Levenson's pawn shop,
Will you take all these flasks for a bailment?
They're good crystal Mary Jane, but what do they hold
for nourishment? Some, ghosts, doctor.

77

There he came again. To argue.
Would it be once more about
the lizards being my devoted
pet, or else, the way his *exequies*
were conducted? A miscarriage,
dear, he shouted. Joe, a pet
is either no one's conception,
nor no one's misconception,
it is a choice. Mine one was
much more: a gift from Lady Gist
to herself, and he was sneakily
murdered...Urered... Jeanette, daring
as you are you'll end up just like him.
It would be a privilege, floating
down the canal and catch my boarding at the Thames.
What else Joe, money?
...Oney, honey we're, we're in arrears.
Forget me not. I'm Lady Fear, no longer.

78

There has been some inked talk
about this mustiness night on the horizon.
 Nobody says anything enchanting,
even the dirt has been moving to the rice
powdered ones, who no longer know
if they do it either for the sake of beauty,
or because of some purifying snow,
like a benediction which strips the peccancy
away. However, we've all been only
impersonating one another under
a rainy stage. Those afraid of the flood
up the streets became challengers of the night;
the ones wielding the knife are now hiding, waiting
for the copper knight, either on the ninth or the tenth
November. Can't remember.
The Master Builder has come to set my clock.

79

In the end,
it simply came up to be as the night of the red shawl.
After the evening of the flower in my head. Also red.
It should all have been in a very dark grey, so to appal
the Albrooks, the Fosters, the Harveys, and the sad
lascivious bug building with an exscinded purple eye,
supervising the passers-by and the girls and the girls.
A dark grey is monstruous ordinarily, but it would tie
the entire rows of or contradictory claims of prayers
to the event. *Grey is so monstruous because there
is no red in it.* From this on, all turned into a red piece.
From the onset, the shawl. Then the flower, first, a spared
white; right after, an insidious red; first, down my Greek
bosom, then upon my head, at last just pinned to a black
jacket. All ended up to be in red, on reddish eyes' fleek
look. My red evening in red singing to a red night match.
If red is in everything it is not necessary.

80

A red to ginger, dark blond to rosy brown bearded
stout fellow, pulled my hand in an illusionist caress;
a kind move out of a circus figure, either to impress
or simply to deliver the warning not to turn a red headed
night into a yellow one. A bile yellow greenish nightshift,
just because I was dancing the streets and having
my songs sang, summoning up all the city into a grift.
There I was taking a mean trick to the fearful craving.
My cheering mood had the gift to let the red night ones
up the grift, just for fun's sake; I let down the black
magic night ones, the others, leaving them to become those
who rather want a bloody than a red night: slag.
Still dancing and singing in the rain. After all, I'm a Kelly.
My hand was harsher pulled. I could only offer a telling
of who he was as I listened to his voice. Wise building's
Master Builder. No choice.

81

What's worth a hand of a whore
In the hand of mortar?
What's the use of having stored
stone fingers under the scratch
of polished red claws?
Was it a match,
Was it the usual catch?
The dancing passed from
hand to arm, arm to shoulder,
then chest to breast.
Finally, from mouth to hear.
Mine on his.
Just for the sake of a clear
gather from a mutc
Master Builder.
It ran not like the story goes.
Instead, it was a breeze
I did blow on him,
Will you, will you not?

82. The Virus Inquest – Part II

You do fill all the complete face card
of a mate quite immune to a contagion.
Would you be most patient as to regard
the entries you must not, in this region
of the city, ever leave sorting behind,
as they do constitute a self-defence
equipment to any misdeed to mind
out and about? To a builder's offense,
used to shields and helmets, do find
in this items, please, a soulful quest.
Collar and cuffs trimmed in astrakhan;
a very thick gold chain, that's of a man.
You've, no doubt, self-made some a million
pounds baskets.
A large seal and a red stone, what a talisman.
Inquest accomplished. Come along. Let us go,
the Magician and I.
Mind my asking,
Are you also familiar to caskets?

83. The Courtcoming

See that bow down arch?
When you'll cross it, you will
have to be up with the lark.
Welcome to Miller's Court,
some say a bill
never a Master Builder is
to be acquainted with. I take
the risk and try the thrill,
also the command, Do make
no comments.
The passage, some say an anus,
gets narrower as you'll get
to the court, in a way, one
has to enter in skewed fret.
Be accurate, twenty-six feet
four inches long, and two feet
ten inches wide. Width to a
ratio less than ten percent
to length. Let's strip some anal
tissue of flesh to see if the canals
match. How funny is that?
Beyond arch and catwalk,

you'll find the bowels.
And the owls.

84

Am I entitled to your visiting
this highly recommended
chamber of mine? I'm only tilting
the door a bit. Alice bended
it askew, now for the sake of two
rabbits, and to avenge Carrol's
fails. She's also up to these roles
of facetious plays,
and wants to strip I don't know who.
Some blue hair queen, I believe.
But first, do pay a look at the oddities
of this open-air setting. Dwarves' lairs
within too whitewashed walls for sensitive
cycs, which turn us all into dizzy moles.
A Sir Alfred has been around, and his
verdict: No use.
However, he mostly was of the porcine type.
By dawn, take your place towards the middle right of it.
A batman will come to help you jump out
up Commercial Street. Or you can do it yourself.

85

The Master Builder's steps
were this tender and quiet
such as he was of the silent kind.
I offered myself to the fore. Clung
onto him, "I am having a song".
Had to repeat it softly, because
he sort of has gotten underwood.
I gathered he's misunderstood
it for "I am having a son".
I did start singing so. Some tune
learnt on mother's grave. It seems
I was too much in a lurch to even
get to a church choir canorously,
"A Violet I Plucked from My
Mother's Grave When a Boy", it ran.
Then I got my first tight hug.
And I also got my first crush.
And after that, my early past tense hungover.
By the end of the night, my ultimate hanging. On. Red.
Just for the matter, Are you familiar to clovers?

86

The Master Builder made it to the chair,
such a dismembered furnishing, that its use,
what a use, could only stand for a torture device; one pair
of window panes with green shutters, miserable ruse,
right behind him; he just turned into a *Sea King's* snatch.
I've sat on the bed's border, hanging legs
with naked feet. I freely felt like a pledged *little match*
girl. I did the honours of the house, No rags,
I'm sorry, but put yourself at ease. At least, take off
your boots. Have you the smelly feet? A peg's
bizarre show admits whatever, such as a chicken stroganoff
rotten pan. Feel free to. He endured a long stare
on the partition wall. I realized he could take a sight
beyond the wood, the frames, the paper, the bare
stuff it was made of, It's the shed out there, I declared.
And a gaslight, with a man beneath it too,
he did reply.
It's just Mr Hutchinson, a client.
As the night will get redder, he'll do the fly
like a shed goose, I sustained.
A client is a customer, is a payer, is a client.
You're used to that, Dear.

Then he diverted his eyes to the picture hanging above the fireplace. Some trinket.

87. The Fisherman's Widow – An Ekphrasis (a)

She stands alone on the right,
walking rather far rightwards.
By these times, in that dashed
dark dress of hers, she's already
run all the way through to the opposite
side of the room, out of the cardboard.
The path offers no difficulty, she just
must keep herself all along the sea-line,
a vanishing edge of horizon, cutting
her figure in two chunks by her elegant
waist. Quite a stripping. She cries
no longer, although you can watch
the beautiful serenity of her mourning
as the attention she pays to the children
on her track is like the one she'd have taken
the care of looking to weasels by her side.
The fisherman's gone, but the infants remained. Playing is
their earning, and they've already
got a harvest basket and a small boat into a miniature.
The burial has been quite a feast, and the future days will
bring no beast. The fisherman's soul has no

retreat, and the children keep up to no
mistreat on their pathfinder, Miss Darkness.
Mr Master Builder took all the time
he needed to on this fancy tell-tale bark.
Or was that any expert analysis?
What for had the landlord McCarthy's brains come upon such
an idea as hanging that printing above the fireplace?
Just to spoil my red night of a crush.
It should have fallen into the flames beneath
much a time ago.

88

I have to save my words, not to fall
into the saddest taste of superlativeness.
Although words are regarded not
to pertain to the considerable personal
attraction I'm supposed to possess. Caught.
Master Builder, my architect,
Master Builder, my painter,
Master Builder, my portraitist.
My recreator, my moulder, my artist.
You've done me like some art movements'
men only will have the guts to do the experiments
half a century ahead this red night session.
What an expression technics haven't you arrange.
What a sketching, what a plan. Haven't you taken
me as your flesh canvas, your living picture
of a still life dead character?
What a cuts, what a strokes. What a touch.
Such an obliqueness of plastic traits,
made of me the first cubistiquist achievement
worth remembering. I'll be your perpetual
Pablo's Dora Maar. Your time and again
Bacon's Innocent X. I'm glad you gave way

to your artistic cravings and took me as material
of such means, only artistry of a century
and a half to come, will be managing to try:
What a happening, what a performance.
Mary Jane, your plaster.
Master Builder, my sculptor.
A masterpiece.

89. Mary Jane Kelly's Wunderkammer – An Ekphrasis (b)

For art's sake and future memory, here stands the record of my Red Night Chamber, Mary Jane Kelly's Cabinet of Curiosities.

An old-school coat
on a window glass hole;
for a curtain roll.
A flesh bundle
faintly skeletal.
A woman's head resting
on her left cheek.
A pair of eyes
bulging out of a skull.
A neck in *ecchymosis*.
Spleen to the left,
fingers clenched.
A two feet square pool
of red foam on the floor.
A dizzy moth as a flying dot.

Enclosed fire.
Ashes.
The door had to be
forced open.

90. The Carotid Elegy

The extreme noble artery
Right wing Lady Carotid
suffered this serendipity;
Searching for a red parrot,
which, from her Aldgate spot,
fled his perch in rapidity,
she ended at Whitechapel's hot
heart. How can a Dignitary
lead herself to that misery lot?
Luckily, she crossed upon a military
who gifted her a piece of cloth
to clean her drained *sanguiny.*
Then he led the Lady to an alley
in order to offer some shortcut
out of the damp vicinity. And he cut.

91

Can you see, Mrs Phoenix,
the untasteful plate
they've put upon me?
Such a metal mounted fate;
brass polished engraved
Marie Jeannette Kelly.
Even the spelling
embarrasses me.
Now, I no longer
know whether I'm
Jeannette, Jeannete
or Jeanette. No, not at all.
I'm Jeanette single 'n'
not Jeannette double 'n'
'Cause Jeanette single 'n'
sounds gin, not gen.
You don't know how
I crave for that old
rusty iron plate, over
the arch bearing
the legend,
'Miller's Court'.

92. Satyriasis

Ginger got to the streets
because she was certain
to come across someone.
The very one whose feet
she was into the follow
must have been pouring
something from a callous
body protuberance; nasty.
She found nothing but pasty
liquid glass and enduring
ice pins. At last, she stepped
upon some bizarries to the touring.
A red astrakhan ascot, dirty
with a creamy fluid, a sugar icing
like cake filling. Did she grab it.
An ice penis was undercover.
She came back
only with a piece
of crystal.
Just for the matter.

93

For a bet, only, Mrs Cox made an offer
to afford her Lady Goose's feathers,
countering that she really saw Mary Jane
smoking under the court's arch, hours later
I had entered for good my mausoleum.
My Private Myth Art Museum.

94

The waiting for the great stratagem
ended to render everybody into a defeat.
*The order for the bloodhounds had been
countermanded.*
The dogs were not sent for.
Am I not having a song, now? I say.
Send in the Clowns.

95

A cortège.
Daring fellow.
All in beige,
I asked. Mellow.
Shoreditch
mortuary.
They're into *kitsch*.
I'm simply Mary.

96

Leytonstone for a bed,
when what I want is a canopy
in Tower Hamlets. Red.
Stratford's Manor for an estuary,
whereas I'd rather go for where
The Regent's Canal marry
the Thames. To meet there
Marie Jeanette's flaky pet.
Father Columban for the last words.
It would suffice my Crystal Lad's voice.

97

Mr H. Wilton, generosity is no
part of this talk.
Paying for a burial, dear Mister,
what is it in compare with paying
for the Master Builder's art?
All for publicity's sake.
Let *the time goes by and you'll*
find no hyperbolic image of
the ever-selling Mary Jane Kelly.
A hyperbole much a mandatory one
not to figure in suspicious poetry:
an elderly woman offered a great sum
of money for a lock of my hair.
I'm sorry, Ma'am, the only person
touching my hair is Mrs Phoenix,
157 Bow Common Lane.

98

Your talks are getting
rarer and rarer, Mary Jane,
Mrs Phoenix's saying.
Is there any little bird around?
I would even sustain
you've been under a mood
most bizarre,
she added.
Nothing's the matter,
I've told her. It's just
that now I've been going
to bed earlier.

99

Awaken by six in the morning,
I went to Mr Levenson
pawn shop, to retrieve
my ghosts on flasks. Done.
Now I'm ready for my fortune
making, Mr Master Builder.